THE ORACLES OF OUR STARS

THE ORACLES OF OUR STARS

Poetry

Serge Elie Seropian

ISBN 978-1-7771404-0-3

Cover design by Arash Jahani.

To Serly
with love

"At that time Jesus said, "I praise You, Father, Lord of heaven and earth, that You have hidden these things from *the* wise and intelligent and have revealed them to infants. Yes, Father, for this way was well-pleasing in Your sight."

Matthew 11: 25-27 NASB

THE ORACLES
OF
OUR STARS

Before we knew each other,
we knew each other
we didn't speak to one another,
yet we spoke to one another,
we hadn't met
but we had known each other this whole time
and in our start we completed each other
with the void that was meant
for each other our whole lives.

⁂

Though we weren't meant to be
  we were meant to meet,

As quick as a fleeting memory of childhood reminisces
Were we to each other,

But we were destined to cross paths,
Even by the hands of God;

Above the stars of the universe,
  We lay as two separate ideas merging;

Two ideas personified by two people, you and me,
  me and you, meeting in the up-springing of our youth
But we were as old as time, even though we were not
aware of it;

Since Fate had us meet in theory before Fate had run its
  decided course,
We met above the stars in Fate's determined thoughts
  even before the manifestation of our meeting took place
on this earth,

And this my youthful love
 has made all the difference to me.

⁂

As for my love,
my reverie is her only remains
But as long as that part of the brain
which enables her remembrance
and that other part, whether
derived from the brain or the heart,
which procreates the art of my poetic verse,
as long as these two are at play and work,
then I can see her again;
although that same reverie causes me
to be out of touch with my world,
because in every turning woman's face,
they turn to look much like hers.

⁂

My poetry is lovely from the sight of her.

⁂

Here is poetry
And here are my rhymes,

And here is the form
Lovely from the sight of her
Altogether lovely,

Altogether stirred with words and heart combined.

⁂

Though I could say
 that you were beautiful
 or that you were smart
I wished you'd let me show you
 that there's more to you
than my words inscribed and
written from a broken heart.

⁂

I'll say
to her:
blossom
  my delicate rose
even though
the rose was never
mine,

As a rose,
  she stood still,
admired by a seer,
and yet she stood blind,

and although her beauty forever remains
refrained from me to see
her lovely clear features, and
her dark uncaring eyes,
she is altogether lovely,
and altogether one kind.

⁂

Often have you heard it said
That Love is blind,
But Love is not blind
When it sees all
And yet loves anyway.

⁂

And when I reminisce, her spirit
Comes to knock on the door of my heart,
And there I can hear her silent thoughts

Are you really that restless?
You traded me so that you'd gain
A lover who lives
In these poetic lines?
Yet in seasons when lovers give,
and while they live, lovers remember the old
As they cling cheers to the new,
But you remain constrained in these lines,
Lacking the love that once nurtured you.

⁂

We were too young to appreciate what we had
even though we felt it,
and at times, we were overwhelmed by it;
but it took some growing to understand,
and some experience to realize how rare that was.

⁂

Darling,
You tried to hide your imperfections from me
but you didn't know how I thought
that it was your imperfections
which made you so beautiful.

⁂

Her dark indifferent heart
Her bright warm heart
I can find my nights and days in them.

⁂

Love loves the flaws.

⁂

And now we have to pretend we hate each other
Because there really is no other way
Where we can fit into each other's lives.

⁂

How can love make sense when
Love resides above the universe?
Love transcends the limits of our minds.

It is for you to feel love
but not for you to elaborate on it any longer

For love is its own poet
And its nature is its poetry.

⁂

Her eyes spoke a language that could captivate you
And she knew she could be your weakness,
And the world knew she couldn't be tied down
And what men most feared in her,
I loved the most.

⁂

Let love break you because

Whether you are guarding yourself from love
in your cold-hearted prudence,
or whether you are opening your arms to love
like a free spirit with an open heart,
love will break you all the same,

And when Love breaks you,
It prunes you,
and its pruning reveals the secrets of Life's teaching
and Life's heart that only Life's secret pupils know,

And in love's teaching, you will break free from yourself
and be closer to God, even as when we die we will die to
ourselves and wander upwards like a spirit uncaged, closer
to God but further from ourselves; when we become
familiar with God we will become
unfamiliar with ourselves, we will live in God when we die
to ourselves;

And to know God, you must first love;
And to know love means you must feel the vulnerability of
love freely and be crushed by it;
When we love we experience a fraction of what God feels
for all of us,
Love is rarely without its heartbreak;

Life's purpose is love, and so you were destined
to be broken by love even as you were destined
to be born; love makes you vulnerable, even as God
is vulnerable by His loving you;

Life is Love made perceptible
You were born because someone loved you.

⁂

"You are a free spirit" the boy said,
"so all who dare to adore you
must adore you as one"

That little boy was me
and you were my beloved.

⁂

If you truly love her, love her free spiritedly,
And if she truly loves you,
She will be loyal to you even when she is a free spirit;
Let love be the only thing that binds you.

⁂

What better love is there than this?
That two souls should be bound by no rules,
nor customs, nor expectations,
but bound solely by the conviction of their love,
which is neither forced, nor asked, but understood silently between
Two souls speaking freely in the language of love.

⁂

A free spirit is not bad,
It is a bird that cannot be caged;
Caging a bird would be selfish and immoral,
Yes, and though you are meant for the ground,
She was meant for the open air,
And to be caressed by the winds
A bird is not evil when it wants to fly, is it?
A lion is not evil when it treads the grounds, is it?
Leave everyone as they were made to be;
And though you find refreshment on the ground,
She finds it in the open air,
Let everyone choose their refreshment for their souls.

⁂

A lion has a demeanor to roar,
but it is in a lamb's disposition to be meek,
And a wolf is to be independent minded and occupy itself in hunting
even from its quick motions even when immersed in the shadows,

A wolf cannot be meek,
A lamb cannot roar,
And neither creature can be a lion,

Everyone has a character and a need,
And when you love,
Choose to love them as they are;
Choose not to change anyone, when you can learn to understand them for who they are;
Do not change anyone, because
every human soul has a need springing from the soul
which is soaring in of itself even to its destination, and from its destination even to eternity
which you cannot grasp nor stop, even if you tried.

⁂

If you were to cut
 a bird's wings
to prevent itself from flying,
 then you are against nature,
and acting on your cruelty,

How much more a human being
 if you tried to tame them?
How much more a human soul
which you cannot tame?

Love your lovers as free spirits,
 even as free winged as a bird in its prime,

If they belong to you, they will come to you, freely, even as their free spirit implies.

⁂

Love loves the flaws
the moral flaws, the inconsistencies in thought,
the quirkiness in the way the beloved speaks and
enunciates certain words;
Love transcends the flaws,
the flaws become a part of the beloved,
And since the beloved is perfect in the eyes of the lover,
the flaws are then perfect.

⁂

In this world,
The most powerful rule over everything,
But love is not from this world,

And hence, love crushes the most powerful,
It traps the rich where their riches cannot save them,
and it leaves the well-known lost in an unfamiliar and dark place

Love perplexes great minds,
and Love makes great minds abandon their natural course
even as great winds have made ships abandon their course,
Great minds will no longer be able to perceive with their minds,
But they will feel the burdened form of crushing within their broken hearts,

Love crushes everyone's heart;
For love, being from above, is too burdensome for the weary heart to carry

And when it brings down the most powerful,
to humble them in a state of nothingness,
Love teaches them Life's secret lessons
which can only be understood when felt,
And remembered when heard.

⁂

Consider everything and everyone as a preparation for the great love
Now the great love is in your hands, and in your true beloved's hands you will be there eternally;
What is your great love but that which you can make your home with as long as you are alive?
What is your great love but a source of eternal refreshment and comfort from the troubles outside?
What is the great love but that which opens you up to know yourself and be who you truly are?
And what is the great love but the shadow of God's love for you?

⁂

You and I were the poetry
That we were not allowed to speak of
And in what was too sacred for utterances,
We expressed in secret with actions of kindness.

⁂

And when I first expressed my love for you,
You were scared as though it were something new
For new things scare people,

The irony in this is true,
For nothing is as it seems,

My darling, I desperately wanted you to know
That nothing would have changed,
And what I expressed before in action
I now also express with words,
And that was the only difference.

⁂

In eternity, when I childishly snuck into
the courtroom of God, I heard God
when He said, "Not with words will I teach you all
compassion, vulnerability, and a forgiveness
that keeps no records of wrongs;
and then I will fill you all with selflessness,
So,
In humble obedience,
Fate has ever decreed that we will all lack
the love that we were once nourished by.

⁂

It's the most confident ones
that are the most broken.

⁂

The human frame is the temple of God
And God resides in the heart.

⁂

Humanity is God's styled architecture
Would you tear down that which He loves?

⁂

Why do you hurt and enslave God's living temple,
in order to create your own empire?
Let us see if God will not tear down your empire.

⁂

The human-body is God's architectural temple
And when men and women take pleasure in the temple's superficial beauty
and evaluates the temple's worth based on the pleasure of their eyes;
God sees the heart, the source of everything,
and evaluates each temple according to the pleasure of His eyes.

⁂

Often have you heard that you must fight
for what you want,
Often have you been taught as though life
is all about fulfilling current desires till it is
no longer unfulfilled or till it is no longer desired;

But I say that Life is not all about what you want,
but the opposite;
Maybe we must forgo what we want only to get
lost on the trail of discoveries and to get lost on
the roads of new meaning to a new place, where
new smiles are seen, where new beautiful
sights appear on the forefront of your horizon,
where a new you will emerge and a new want
fulfilled.

⁂

Do not lose your heart nor your soul
For the hardened world will be gone
tomorrow;

Let the world laugh in all its wickedness
Let the world laugh with all their evil plans
For the hardened world will be gone
tomorrow;

I let the world do evil things to me,
And I neither retaliate
Nor seek revenge
For the hardened world will be gone
tomorrow;

So do not harden your heart; do not join
  in the world's wickedness,
For the hardened world will be gone
tomorrow;

Take no refuge in the wickedness of this
world,
For the hardened world will be gone
tomorrow;

Do not lose yourself;
But find your soul in the palm of your creator,
For the hardened world will be gone
tomorrow;

I let the world judge me for my non-retaliation
I let them say "Look here at a person who does
Not belong to this world and has neither worldly
Wisdom nor worldly understanding,"
But in a silent understanding,
and with my starry-eyed stare

and with a non-response
that is deemed to be incompetence,
I know
that the hardened world will be gone tomorrow.

⁂

In this world, everything is presented before you
 for a price;
but this is not the case with God,
 who created the world freely, and gave it to you, freely,

Therefore, give to everyone who asks from you,
give and ask for nothing in return,
give and expect nothing in return,
for then you will be conjoined with God in God's loving,

You are meant to overcome the world, and as a soldier
marching into battle, ready for the war that
many before you have fought;
and the war many after you will fight;
you will be embraced and placed among high ranks,
you will join heavenly places
and be filled with heavenly graces;
you will shine brighter than the sun;

You are meant to overcome the world,
so do not imitate the world
that presently causes sorrow and is passing tomorrow;
but imitate your father in heaven,
and you will become children of God.

⁂

And your heartbreak in my absence became
my heartbreak in yours.

⁂

I adored your quirkiness; it was what made you unique,

I adored it to the point that I absorbed it in my mind,
and in my heart, it then became a part of me.
Two souls and two personalities embodied in me.

Till this day I carry you with me,
I talk the way you do at times,
That's the effect you've had on me.

And I may not have any intention of carrying you with me,
but I do, subconsciously,

And it all started with a little smirk upon my face
When I would look at you in astonishment at the way
You'd pronounce certain words,

You were my dorky and eccentric love
and yet you were so cool.

⁂

I loved you with that kind of love
that can only be described in movies and books
and that only ends in heartbreak.

⁂

If I could tell you one thing, as I lay in my bed with you,
admiring every moment I get to be near you,
worshipping you even from the depths of my spirit,

As I reach out to touch you, I want you
to look at my eyes which reflect the goddess whom I worship,

But even my presence would reveal that I am in awe of you
for I have never been so cautious as to be so meticulous and slow,
respectful from the depths of my soul, reminding myself to take in
every moment;

If I could tell you one thing
it would be
that I want to melt away and be a running brook
that loses itself to be in your slender arms
and to be the reason you smile from your heart's embrace,
every time you smile, I want to be the reason why, and I want to lose myself to be in you;

As we lay in my bed I want you to look and see
how vulnerable my eyes are when I look at you,
I want you to know that I was born to live but I'd rather die here with you;

You could kill me if you want to, because I handed my life over to you, trusting you, that you would not want to, trusting the idea that you would not want to, but yet I know that you could kill me,
and that I would not hold it against you, if you did; "please don't my life is in your hands" I would say you are my

weakness and in your presence my strength melts, I lay emotionally threadbare in my bed with you as a mortal man in love with a goddess.

⁂

Know that while you live,
You ought to embrace the still-quietness of life
Although it be a gift unknown to many;

In solitude, unfold your memories
and embrace them
Even though the quiet life makes you unloved by many;
And Joseph was not loved so long as he was a dreamer;

Indeed your memories are your muses,
So long as you forsake them not,
They will always be eager to impart
Gifts to yourselves;

And even though your muses' motives
To teach you may be hidden,
Harken to them as teachers in silence;

What have I to say to this world other than
That it should slow down to win the race,
To contemplate the many lessons of musings,
The lessons which would really put you ahead
Even with a slower and more becoming pace;

If only for you, reveries were sweet enough
To indulge in more; and then you will find
That memories are fairly valued
Like wine, when we esteem them
Of greater worth with passing time
And better their taste for you when your time is declining,
And despite this, you are in most need of them
When you are young and when they are but bitter

teachers;

Yes and recall how memories are both sweet and bitter
And without contradiction,
And, you should look to them more
Than the present situation or the hopeful future,
Because in them you may find many hidden treasures
Although they appear as miscellaneous items;
Yes, in them are many beautiful sceneries,
Although they are as hidden doorways to the untaught eye;
And as to the unlearned only
Do letters and words appear as jargon,
But in them can either life or death be found,
Just so are memories,
And just so is poetry;

Though it remains a gift unknown to many,
The still-quietness of life is the only gift
In which you should look upon your memories;

If only reveries would rouse you
To be dreamers in this world;

Be dreamers in this world
So that you would find
The experiences of your life,
As when the first of lovers met
And when you kissed your beloved with your heart
And when your beloved embraced you with loving arms
Remember them, as in the wake, that life is one fleeting memory,
For it is but a dream and we are but dreamers;
Remember them as a refreshment to your soul

As new wine to your carnal taste
As a wave, stimulating your soul, the core of your being;

And sometimes you would find
The merry laughter of simplicity
With the cherishing of the likeminded
Whom you've crowned with the title of "friend"
And for whom you've split your own soul
So you could share it with her or with him
So that you could spend your days with her or with him;

And sometimes you would find
The brutality of life
Which first introduced itself to you
When it first shattered you
And plucked the hairs out of your head
And protruded tears out of your eyes
As you would the sap of a fruit
Remember that the earth is a tree
And you are its first fruits;

So when memories grants you pain
Consider that together you ride the wave
With the lilies and the fruit-trees
And together you will fade
Together you freely enjoy the caressing wind
And together will you be sifted apart by it;
So enjoy in your memories their atmosphere and their feeling
For altogether with their sound and image they are fleeting
even in the silence you train yourself to enjoy;

And sometimes you would
Just have to welcome
Some meaningless memories,
But their meaninglessness would cheaply mimic
Reluctant children who do
Budge when its parent, Time, raises them up to
purposefulness;
And just as wine is esteemed of greater worth
With the passage of time,
So the sweetness of a memory's meaning is known to you
Only through your growth;

And yes remember the
Memories that did hurt you
Even though without reason did they hurt you
In this random process of living;
Even embrace the meaningless events simmering
In the fogginess of your head and

Choose not to remember the good memories exclusively
from now on,
Even though you thought these meaningless memories
Were but the shadows of vanity,
As long as you are alive,
The breath of life is not so short of breath
So as to hide the purpose of their visit;
And while many are the lessons yet to be uncovered
From them,
Consider that a memory's meaning will come to you
When you are not adamantly searching for it,
So consider the musings of your heart and of your mind
but
Not as a searcher of treasures nor a searcher of meaning,
But as a traveller who indulges in travels,
As travellers that do enjoy the journeys set before them,

For many are your Tutor's lessons hidden
In memories as they are in travels,
And God's voice and God's hand can be but revealed in them
And many are the destroyed relics that point to its fuller picture.

⁂

You have heard it was said
Fear comes by considering reality
But I say that
Fear is a false emotion turned into a reality
And fear caused you to lose:
The woman you never pursued
Even though she had your heart knitted in hers;
And fear caused you to lose:
The dream you never learned to pursue
As you wake daily to proceed with the occupation you never loved
Yeah, the occupation you never loved which
You turned into your career up until your deathbed;

Fear caused you to lose:
The progression you never pursued
Being content with your current success
Even as it fades past you beyond existence
You were content with your success
Because you did not believe it would last
Nor that you would progress;

So fear has brought you nothing but realities
First shaped by your own imaginings
So be bold even though you may think boldness
Has no settlement in you,
Be yourself without providing an explanation
As to why you are the way you are,
And live your life the way it ought to be lived
And do not be afraid.

⁂

Those who are in need to receive love,
receive;
Those who are in need to give love,
give;
And those who are in need to give love
without receiving will receive the love of
God.

⁂

If in your heart you can replace them,
then darling, it is not love.
If from your mind you can erase them,
then darling, it is not love.
And if with your soul, you can forsake them,
then darling, it is not love.
It is not love, it is not love
Darling, if you want to argue with me,
Then you do not love;

For even when you do forsake them,
a part of you will always want to come back
and that wanting through time repressed will
become a need; and that need will burst forth
from your insanity,

And if you do not go insane,
then darling, it is not love,

If you do not replicate their image in every person you see
by the complex processes of your brain,
then darling, it is not love.
It is not love, it is not love,
Darling, if you want to argue with me,
You are not in love,

For love stays even when you will it to leave;
Love will not go away, even when you plead
And find someone else who will not impress
themselves on yourself that strong
For you've learned your lessons
And from youthful fantasies
You've moved on.

⁂

Love my dear,
Love is the reason why we are here,

And so when you encounter Love,
Then you will understand that Love is the vine
And you are a twig broken off a loveless tree
And grafted into the vine of Love;

Love will bear much fruit in you
But first you must be broken;

And this is why you are here,
to be grafted into the vine of love
to let it nourish you unto everlasting life
to let it remake you in the newness of its life
to let it love and teach you how to love
before you depart from the cursed loveless world
and enter into the kingdom of heaven where love resides.

⁂

There are somethings that only the heart can fix.

⁂

There is so much suffering in the world,
So why should I desire to be the cause of your suffering?

You've already suffered so much in your life, and more suffering is hidden in the dark bushes among your path that you have yet to see; so why should I also add to your suffering cup?

Oh my enemies, how can I hate you when I see myself in you?

How can I hate you when you are just as fragile to life's fragilities as I am? To old age, to sickness and to death like I am?

⁂

My worth is not based on human judgement.

⁂

You are a seed planted in the earth
And in the astonishment of your enemies
you will grow

And when you reach the heights of your
success; all will marvel at your honor and
your beauty,

Yes, even you will be astonished though
you know it in your soul that it will come to
be true,

And this is why you work hard because, in
your thoughts you say, that you may hasten that day.

And while you grow, you will enjoy
your growth, and when you reach the heights
of your success, you will be satisfied, for a time;
But, one warning lays ahead of you, and
this you should know:

That if you had all the beauty in the world,
but if you did not learn to love even with all
the beauty in the world,
then you are a seed grown to astonish only
for a short time,

Yes, you will grow to be an orchard of apple trees
that will be cut down and whose fruits
were never tasted and your beauty would be taken,

The bark of your trees will be thrown into
the fire, and your yesterdays will no longer
be remembered, your present will no longer be felt,
Your future is no longer seen –

Your beauty, your gifts and your hard work will fade
And separation from life is the price that you've paid
if you did not learn how to love.

⁂

You will look for me
But you will not find me.

⁂

Why impress the world with its
pretensions beloved?

⁂

Yes I say to you be careful
of how you treat her because
a time may come in the near future
that will feel like tomorrow
where you will look for her
but will not be able
to find her.

⁂

And if they do not see the good in you
It is because they were not meant to.

⁂

If I break your heart,
I break my heart
For my heart is linked to your heart and
Your heart is mine,

When your soul aches
  my soul aches
for we are tied together in
the sympathies and compassion
of love,

When you are let down
  my soul aches
more than tears can show
and much more lasting than tears;
much more permanent than
physical pain,

How can I ever be deliberately rude or
  malicious to you darling, when you are
linked to my heart and my soul – when you
are my vulnerability?

⁂

You already know everything
And yet you look for teachers.

⁂

When I first saw her, I loved the way she looked
and yet I know I love her painter's soul more when she
speaks;
she paints a canvas with her words,

What's happening to me? Should I stare or should I
retreat;
no, I'll stare; and look away and muster more courage to
its peak;
coming to you but you had come over me before you ever
knew what
it was like; this kind of movie love, this book love, this
fairy-tale that people make fun of;

And often do people make fun of what they do not know,
and that they'll never understand; but I feel it in my heart,
so I know it is true; even though I knew that the stars had
other plans;

So when you loved me, I no longer wanted to be with you,
though I loved you still; for while I loved you too early,
you loved me too late; and this was the difference that
made our love lose its stakes;

So by the time you spoke up for me, I was already running
away, thinking that I'd store these memories as fond
memories one day;
that despite your heart's welcome I knew in my soul that I
shouldn't stay;

For even as these stars destined us to love each other;
These same stars destined that we ought never be
together,

So do not hold it against me; I loved you with all my heart
in all its purity, and unconditionally; but I couldn't love

you when the time for my loving you was up and when our time was never; you had something coming along that you would later realize is better;

So do not hold a grudge against me because that feeling I also know, and I know it with all my heart; to love really well hurts when that which you love must soon depart.

⁂

Love is found by those
who do not search for it.

⁂

Among women,
You were the most beautiful I had ever seen
and ever known
and I know I'll never get to see you again,
and if I do, it'll be as if we never met,

That quirky way you pronounced certain words I'll
never hear again
And as for your beautiful voice
I'll never hear your sound again
I miss the way you walked
and the way you smiled and looked happy in
sunny days of simple youth that I'll
never see again,

What more can I say beloved? I'm sorry
I put an end to our relationship because
I ended a part of you, and in that,
I ended a part of me,
Which I'll never feel again,

I'm sorry that I put an end to my loving you,
for you'll never feel me adore you with my
whole heart again; you'll never feel
my hand caress your hair and your skin like I
wanted to back then,

And even though there are many men you can find to
replace me on that; but I promise you they would
never do it with a worshipping spirit like I do;
and this is why I am sorry; for it is true that love
makes simple moments magic, which, out of my
cautiousness I prohibited you from.

⁂

When I saw you
there were a thousand
unexpressed feelings
weighing on me
disabling me from speaking.

⁂

Oh Lebanon, must the blind judge your beauty? Or
the deaf the sound of your voice?
Should you enslave yourself to those whom you deem as
primitive and lacking in many ways?
Though meek and mild, should you be ruled by
tyrants? Compassionate and yet ruled by
compassionless men?
How should the dead tell us how to live?
The past is buried and their rulers with them;
Lebanon will rise with love in its heart, and will
extend to the nations their love of life.
Like a branch extending forth its ripe fruit,
You will extend your hand, and all will try
Your goodness, and all will know that you are
the beauty of nations.

⁂

Revenge consumes those who seek it
Free yourself from such a master.

⁂

In our silence
There were a thousand
Unexpressed feelings
Because our spirits knew
That words are unnecessary
In this place
Where feelings are felt
One by another
And talk all on their own.

⁂

When you judge others
You are judging yourself

And when you forgive others,
You are forgiving yourself.

When you forgive others,
You are allowing God to forgive you.
For in the same way you show mercy, you will receive mercy.

⁂

You do not go out to find love
It is love that goes out to find you

And you have not chosen to love one another,
For it is Love that has made you chosen ones;

And we do not create the situation for Love
But rather Love has set an appointed time to introduce itself,

And while Love does knock out of politeness, its presence intends to break the impenetrable forces of your hut;

For Love has come to have its way with you,
It will neither conform to your expectations nor will it meet your demands, for Love is greater than us, and has come to take you up to heaven, to transcend your thoughts, and to transcend your nature;

⁂

Jonathan loved David because Jonathan saw David in himself; for what is a friend but that which you see your own self as? Indeed, those who have not found friends have not found themselves first,

So while the riches of King Saul, which were fading, represent the temporary reign of the carnal self, King Saul told his son Jonathan that he is going to kill David. Indeed, Saul represents the carnality of humanity which will fade and will inherit no lasting glory; but David represents the spirit, which has eternal glory, to surpass the world of the carnal self. And for that, King Saul was jealous of David. Even so, your flesh is jealous of the glory your spirit could inherit, and it tries to put your spirit out. Even in the king's diminishing glory and riches, Jonathan would not allow Saul to kill David; what does Jonathan represent here if not the good friend you have in God?

So I would tell you of the riches that the rich do not know of in the riches of friendship;
For as many as a true friend you have,
Their accommodations in your time of need
Is worth more than your bountiful provisions
In your time of boastful extravagance,
Where you will drink plenty and eat plenty
At a time when you have no need of them;
Truly, your friend's provisions in your time of need
Is but a welcoming hand faintly familiar to family
And even better;

Know that Joy was closer to true friendship
Than it ever was to money,
And if the reverse was ever true
You would find yourself in a lifeless and bland world
Where you will try to satisfy your thirst with eating

Where your thirst is never quenched
And where you will try to satisfy your hunger with drinking
Where your hunger is never satisfied;
Just so will you try to satisfy your void with money
Where you will never have enough to satiate your inner desire,
And haven't even the brightest human beings fallen in that trap?

But I say you ought to cherish your friend,
But I ought never to say that it is because of materialistic gain,
For your friend nourishes your soul first,
Those who have not found friends,
Have not found themselves first,
Indeed those who have not found friends
Have not found their souls first,
Because a gardener points to a garden,
And that which is not a garden
Has no gardener;

But remember that even a wasteland
Can be turned into the greatest orchard
Arranged even by many flowers
As a crown of wreaths on its head,
Even so can a soul-less and lost person
Be cultivated into a soul-full person
With the true friend of vision and heart;

And as many as you have these friends,
These rare friends which money
Can faintly mimic
By means of a cheap thread
Although it is priced too highly,
These friends, you can sing your song to

In your time of distress, you can rely on them,
And although they are few,
They are enough;

And this is the joy that gold can never supply
In its truest form;
And if gold represents superficial fortunes
That is as whimsical as it is shiny,
Then what is gold but an un-loyal person
Who goes to the young and the foolhardy.
The young and foolhardy that you once were
When fortune paid you with its visit?

What is gold but an un-loyal person
Endowed with the lusts it chases
Compared to a loyal friend
Whom you've crowned with trust?

What can we liken gold to but a deceitful person
Who deceives you with empty words
And promises of eternal refreshing streams
That are, in truth, just vacant banks

For the ones that understand this
And have the friendship that I speak of,
They are truly rich, and
They do not lack anything
Even when Life comes to bind them
To drag them down
To their roots
To shake them.

⁂

When King David was in peace
He thought he ought to honor God
By building Him a temple wherein He may reside
To be with David and to be with His people

"Look at me, living in a palace,
While God is living in a lowly tent;"

So too we think that we ought to honor God in this way,
with our own deeds and with our own thoughts,

But the prophet Nathan spoke the words of God, saying:

If only you were willing to do me honor the way I please
And not the way you please from your human sense;
If only you were willing to see the world as I see it
 and not the way you see it
If only you would understand like I do
Then you would be a lasting pleasure to my mind
and then you will bring delight to my heart
more than any passing temple, house, or palace
made of cedar, gold, or bronze;"

David is the spirited person quickened by
the will to do God's will, though his mind does not know
how;
Desiring to do good, but without proper understanding,
prior to revelation.

And God said:

If only you were willing to ask me to build you a house
where you and I would reside and be together
permanently;

Instead of desiring to build me a house, it would be better if I built you one;
If only you were willing to pray that I build a house in you that I may enter in, to do you greater honor than that which you planned to do for me; and I would be with you as a father and a friend;

If only you would say "God enter through the door of my heart, enter through the door of my mind and heart,
and build a house in me
where you live permanently
and then I would have a confidence and a hope that shall not fail
and then I would not be lonely even when the world deems me lonely
and then I would know of the quiet joy distilled even in heartache and in sorrows
and I would have a permanent joy even in the world's hardships.

⁂

Oh you who are broken hearted
Why do you seek to make your faces happy
When your heart is in pain?
When Life deems it for you to walk on nature's thorns
Must you really pretend that you walk on nature's pastures?
And when Life offers you a crooked well to drink from,
Should you refuse to drag from the well
Because of the crookedness of its passageways?
If only you would desire to walk in the miserable way of Life at the time you were called to walk in it,
So that in heartache and in sorrow
You may then know of the quiet joy distilled even in sorrow.

⁂

Those who only look in themselves,
will inherit nothing,
even if they search with all their hearts.

⁂

Alas, hardened hearts will inherit sadness
for when a rock can neither feel nor see,
then how shall their hearts meet God?

⁂

My best friend and lover
I know we've grown apart
But memories of you
Still remain in my heart

I remember them
Like shattered glass
Revealing pieces
of our past

Remember how when
We walked together?
Even then I felt
That we wouldn't last

I remember your smile
And yet your voice
Remains lost

Sometimes it's all a blur,
I bet I wouldn't recognize her
When she's changed,

And we all go through a cycle of
Death and rebirth
I just wish we could have said goodbye
Properly first

Why hold a grudge against me
When I was young
And deny me the closure
Of our nights
Which we spent in fantasy
When reality was right.

⁂

If you were to caress her hair,
do it with love.

And if you were to listen to her speak,
listen to her with your heart's rushing
attendance

And if you were to speak to her,
speak to her with love's soft-spoken tone

In anything,
Let your heart be your motive.

And if you spend time with her by sitting
on green pastures, let love embrace the two of you,
And change your inner beings; so that through your inner
perceptions changed,
You may finally see colors that were previously not
present
From emotions that were previously not felt
Almost as though a new world were opened to you
through a creative pathway shaped like a portal in the sky;

Love her as though life's purpose is loving something so
much you'd lose yourself for it,
for what would it profit you if you never loved and never
entered into the realm of love?
For how does it profit you when you never have
something to lose?

If you feel love come up from your inner being, do not
suppress it;
But if you were to kiss her, then do it with your heart, and
if you were to look upon her, look upon her with loving
eyes,
And if you were to embrace her with your arms, make her

feel your hearts warmth also, for she is worth the love you give; and love in turn will open blind eyes and will heal your ill-patches and perfect
your imperfections.

But if you cannot do this instinctually,
and if love does not naturally spring up from your inner person, then it is better to let her free, for someone will find her, who will give her the love she needs.

⁂

That broken heart of yours
It can do wonders;
Listen to its
Heart-filled melody.

A broken heart is a new beginning.

Direct your broken heart
Into the pathway of your life
And your life's career,
And you will find
That your broken heart
is a remedy to others
Your broken heart
Will change the world.

⁂

When God has called your soul up for royal robes
Why deem yourself a lowly person?

Why follow the evil and malice of people below
When God called your soul up for above,
To think and act above malice, above pride,
Above yourself,

So when someone wrongs you,
Say in your heart "I pity you for you
are enslaved to your wrongs.
Your soul is oppressed and cannot break free
from your carnality by which you've emulated
the evil of the world, as a lost child trying to fit in,
and you've lost yourself more when you have fit in."

"You wrong me, but I desire to do you no wrong.
For you are deceived in thinking that wronging me
Will make you benefit. You feed your carnal cage
with material things that are empty things. Though
you did me wrong, you did me no wrong; for no one
can do me wrong except for God. But you did yourself
wrong, and for that I give you my compassion"

Call up to God, and utter "as surely as you have called me, let my spirit be free. Let it go up to you, and then let your spirit come down to me. For then I need you while I am here, as a child in need of the father who brought us here. I don't know where to go, and I don't know what to do, But I know that you do. I'll live with my royal soul which you've clothed with royal robes; and as for this carnal cage, it is always a peasant even when we design it with the best clothes of earthly peasantry"

The people of their carnality and the people of their souls have this difference among them. It is a vast difference, between consistent joy and persistent depression, between compassion and enmity, love and hate, life and death.

⁂

Your soul is meant for love and compassion
It is filled with compassion and love,

If you desire popularity or riches, the more you strive for it, the more you receive it; but before you pursue these things, consider these are hollow things and will not give you joy though you strive for it with all your heart and even though you receive more than your fair share from your yesterdays.

If you strive for your love and compassion,
You strive for your soul's pursuit, and this
Will bring you true joy,
even if you had no dime, even if you had no friend.

For when you are honest with yourself,
you will have a peace that all enemies
in the world cannot put out.
For if you remain pure and untainted, and
if you strive for your soul's pursuit, you will
bear an honest conscience, and you will never suffer
turbulence.

For the turbulence of the world is outward as the storms of the sea; but if the soul were shaken, how can you have anything substantial without your foundation?

Strive to be your inner person, which is your soul,
which is filled with compassion and love;
For if you forsake this to fit in with the inhumane world,
then you would do yourself no service when you would
strive to put your soul out of its loving flames, you would
but sell your soul as Joseph's brothers sold him into
slavery; you would suppress your soul as King Saul tried to
suppress David.

How then would your soul live happy while in bondage to the evil carnal self? And how can your carnal self live with itself knowing it sold its kin into slavery? For before you receive or give compassion and love, you must first be reconciled to yourself.

⁂

Those who fear life seek to control everything;
But do not fear life and
do not desire to control a thing from now on;
But rather, let Life be in control; ease your mind
and ease your burdens away;
Be a wave in the ocean, kneading pliantly
to the direction of the wind;
For to lose control is the beginning of life
and to understand that your life is not your own
is the beginning of purpose and of wisdom

⁂

When Life offers you to drink from the fountain of his wisdom,
Listen to him and drink from his waters,
And when you hear him with your ears
Hear him with your heart also.

If only you would harken unto your souls
More than you would look for teachers,
For one is truly a teacher
And it has all the answers
Which neither mind nor heart can grasp,
For the breath of God is in you,
and that Life would but give you advice
In the time of your distress.

In truth you depend on others when you do not depend on yourself; but this should not be the case; for whatever is freely given to them
Is also freely given to you, and that which you hear springing from their souls, you can hear springing from your soul.
And if you would but shut your eyes and listen to your soul reveal its intuition in your time of distress,
Then you would be given the advice you need at the time when you most need it.

Then you would realize that you are not alone
Even in your solitude,
And that we are all related by our living.

⁂

Not everything is supposed to be grasped with the mind
But some things can only be grasped with the heart
And others only with the soul.

⁂

When you wonder why a void has come upon you
And within yourself, you feel that there is a goal unmet,
Like an accomplishment eagerly waving at you
Even though you neglect it every day;
"Remember me" says Life,

When you feel hopeless, know that
your purpose is greater than yourself
Since it is not your purpose
but Life's purpose for you,

"Remember me" says Life, "And you will no longer be
hopeless"

And when sorrows come upon you,
Know that sorrows are a means to an end
And not the end, for sorrows give us character
even as a blacksmith gives a blade its character.

"Consider the trees, how they give with no thought in
return" says Life
Trees have yielded to Life's purpose and they bless us with
our air
Must they know their purpose and you not know yours?

When I was younger, my heart was filled with sorrow,
and looking up to the sky, I said "Why me? And why am I
here?
Why these pointless sorrows in my heart?" I said as I shed
many tears,
Looking down defeated with my broken heart, which
is now the cure for many broken hearts.

Deny your purpose if you want, though I know you have
one; deny your purpose if you want, but as for me I know

that:
Even as David remedied the king with his lyre
I'll play with my words and turn fears to liars

This is enough for me,
For even as the trees
Give with no thought in return, I'll do this
Lest inwardly burn.

⁂

Whoever says they have something to boast about,
have nothing to boast about;
For when you claim you have something,
Examine first who you are trying to convince
And why?

If you truly had something you would neither need
to convince yourself nor your friends;
And you would not be seeking for their approval.

⁂

While we are here,
Let us be mindful to the quiet life
When it gives us a mind-full of visitations

And while our hearts are still soft enough to hear
I ask you,
Who do you think of,
When the still quietness of life
Pays you his visit?

Choose not to be ashamed when your thoughts embody
The person that it does; instead, remember to
Hear the angel of visitations, because
Her voice is nothing to be scared of.

And reminisce in the situation which
is no longer – though – it once was;
Because everything visible fades,
And sooner or later time takes us apart;
As what was once notable
Is now just a faded note:

For even when we are separated
From the ones we love,
As time places us in various places
In spheres of dissimilar interests,
The pulse of our hearts still beat likewise,
That part is now as it always was.

Who do you think of
When the still quietness of life
Pays you with its many visits?

And do not be ashamed when your reveries
Embody the person that it does
Or the situation you once loved
And cherished as unperishable.

This quiet prompt invites you on a trip
To know your minds
And in so knowing, you will know yourself,
And in knowing yourself, you will know
Your heart's keepers.

And from time to another
Welcome your mind
So that your mind may reveal
the hidden secrets of your heart

And so when the one who persists to give you a visit
Is no longer locked away in the secrecy of your nature
Show them their visit is welcome in your heart
Even by their sole crossing paths to your thoughts,
Which you've enabled them to,
Even far after they were gone.
And let their away-ness be forgiven,
As though all has been the same
And nothing's changed.
Be accustomed to a forgiveness
That is beyond the record keeping
Of every sin and every mistake;

While sometimes,
Some trivial blur may greatly affect you
And prevent you from seeing that nothings changed all along,
Except for the renewal of our minds,
And the perception of our hearts,
And the anointing that falls on the earth

As our heads cannot maintain all of it in part
And nothing's essentially changed and neither have we
But the little change that will occur is only for the better,
For God would not permit us
To live in a falling world forever.

And ask the ones you think of
For their forgiveness
And they will respond
With positive replies;
And remember them with a carefree love
That is beyond the reflection
Of the times they did wrong,
And the times they did right.

Now let us be accustomed to the angels
Where they know of a love that is, to us, an otherworldly love,
They are out of this world
And so are you, meditating in this sphere
Which you are unaccustomed to.

This invites you on a trip
To know your minds
And in so knowing, you will know yourself
And in knowing yourself, you will know
Your heart's keepers.
And in knowing, there is no fear,
So allow honesty to embellish
The liveliness of your heart
And be honest to yourself before
Your honesty extends to the world,
For in honesty and in plainness,
Nothing will be unknown,
The inner wars that arise from
The fear of the unknown

Will no longer arise,
And there we will know
That in the thoughts which we hid
From ourselves, these have been revealed,
And there was nothing to fear.

⁂

Remember that the most vulnerable in the room
Is the most powerful
And the one who masks their pain the most
Is the weakest though they may show the appearance
Of one that is the most powerful

For who here among you can claim
That you do not mask your own weaknesses?
And why do you do that?
So that you may cower at the adversity
That Life sets in front of you,
And hide yourself so as to give
A version of yourself that your very own
Heart is not even acquainted with?

And indeed, those who know themselves
Are powerful, for they know their strengths and weaknesses
Only to improve upon their weaknesses
And to use their strengths,
So they do not rely on others too much;
For, they rely on themselves
And to know yourself
You ought but to spend time alone,
And when you know yourself
You will also know your heart's keepers;

But if you desire to be strong,
Then be vulnerable,
And express yourself honestly,
For a charismatic leader is a leader
Who first leads themselves out of their-selves before they guide their followers
On how they ought to lead themselves away from darkness,

And yes, be vulnerable,
For to be so would be truthful,
For we are all vulnerable,
But we all cannot admit it openly
For that takes courage and strength.

⁂

Live without expecting that life should be granted to you nor yield to your expectations.
For when you live knowing you are not entitled to life,
Then you ought to know the bliss derived in every pleasure from every seed you gather
And from every fruit you bite,
And in every movement you are allowed for exploration;
And every face you meet along the way is a becoming companion to your heart,
And every smile you face is but a privilege in seeing,
And the person next to you is but a joy shared,
Whose heart-pains are also shared.
Thank Life that you can encounter both pain and joy,
Because a time is coming when you can encounter neither.
For truly, if you knew the pathway, and if you truly had understanding,
Then you would not be jealous of one another.
Then you would not compete so as to kill and to destroy.
Then you would not gossip about another person's shortcomings.
Then you would not fabricate your achievements and fabricate the falls of other people.
Then you would not think that you are smart because of your selfishness
Nor would you think you are smart because of your self-preservation.
Then you would not see the victory in your selfishness
Neither would you see the victory in your self-preservation out of selfish gain.
You would see that your self-preservation is but a fabricated safety that
Disenabled you from Life's birth and Life's growth.
For in the end, we all decay.

But what will the reasons for your death and life be?
And what will you be remembered as?

⁂

Consider the reflection of your face
Know that the complexity of your being
Is evident even from your face's
Superficial details,
Of your eyebrows and their alignment
Of your skin and their pores
Do you believe your complex design
Is only for your outward self?

Do you believe that
Your inward self has no equal complexity,
Detail and meaning?
Do you know of the potential in you
That eagerly waits for your introduction?
If only you would listen to the inner voice within yourself.

Know this,
That greater are they who see your potential before you do,
Greater are they who understand this about you
Before your reach the heights of your success
Where the world will finally approve of you
At a time when you no longer need their approval;
And in that time, you will tend to the outward
Self which you use and manipulate
To express your inward self,
Greater, then, is your inward self
Rather than your outward self,
For the world sees your outward self
And judges you accordingly
But you may judge yourself
According to your inward self,

And within the revealing of the inner core
Among two people, or a few people, or more
There lies the revelry of friendship and the sharing of true spiritual gifts
But when you have not encountered your inward self
You should not judge yourself
Nor should you let the world's judgement of your
Outward self shake you like
An abandoned snake that hides in the dust.

⁂

When Joseph told his brothers he dreamt of being a king
where even his brothers would respect his sovereignty;
and though his father loved him, even his father rebuked
him saying "Shall your mother and I bow down to you
too?"

What can we learn from this story other than
That it is better not to tell people about your dreams
For the world may judge you for what you are
But they will never see you for what you will become;

Hush their empty words; and say,

"You see my flesh, but you do not see my soul".
"You see me now, but later I will triumph like David
triumphed over Goliath, and against all odds – defying
even your expectation."

⁂

Those who know God, have love in their hearts;
Those who know love, have vulnerability as seen by their actions,

These three are as the roots,
and the bark,
and the boughs of a tree,

And if any one of these is cut off, then the fruit tree is not reliable for it can no longer yield its fruits to the earth.

But even as the inner barks are nourished, so the inner soul must be nourished with love. For this is not empty matter; but it is a loving matter. And to give love is easy when God is pouring in your cup.

⁂

Oh, you poor,
Rejoice in your poverty,
For in your poverty,
Jesus did dwell also;
And the apostles were born into a poverty
Which they desired not to escape from except by their untimely deaths,

Yeah, David was a poor boy, a shepherd tending his sheep, when God called him to be king, so that you would know that the poor were destined to do great things.

The poor were chosen to bear God and dwell with God
And among them lies His wisdom which is neither present nor consistent with the rich

Yes, out of the poverty of the poor that are rich in heart, or great in mind, or whole in spirit,
Out of the poverty of such poor ones hides heavenly wisdom clothed in lowly clothing, with a meek smile, and a posture that is unassuming.

⁂

You will find that ones that are connected with God will not say words such as "vengeance" or "justice".
For much of your justice is vengeance disguised, and there is no justice in the world;
Why seek it when you know you'll be wasting your time?

Do us wrong, we will not wrong you in return. We would but pray for you since we know you have no peace in your hearts. We do but have compassion on you as siblings do to their lost siblings.

If you hurl insults on me, it is not you who hurls insults on me, but the spiritual adversary through you who hurls them; for he is trying to get me to hurl insults back at the one he has given reasons to hate.
But I am in the heart of Christ who has enabled me to see the spiritual worlds behind the physical world.
And for this reason, I hurl no insults at you, for I know the spiritual adversary tries to derail me from the path of Christ who does not see his enemies as his enemies, and who desires to give love to anyone that would receive it.
For what is the purpose of life if not to give love? And through love, to animate things which are inanimate, and to resurrect that which is dead, and to find that which is lost.

⁂

Printed in Great Britain
by Amazon

29072351R00071